Sugar Spun Lies

Alexandra Kirk

BookLeaf Publishing

Presentation by *BookLeaf Publishing*

Web: www.bookleafpub.com

E-mail: info@bookleafpub.com

ISBN: 9789357211857

First edition 2023

DEDICATION

For Ben, you always believed in me

Love was/Love is

Love was sugar spun lies, blood on the knife
edge
Love was the jump
Love was her running down the hallway and
leaping into my arms
Love was a cut in a dark room
Love was red with blood
Love was written in letters, journals, mix tapes
and on my skin.
Love was jumping off the end of her/my rope

Love is listening to his music through
headphones while he sleeps
Love is lying next to him in pain, without hope
Love is addiction, not being able to say no
Love is messages in the morning and kisses
goodnight.
Love is magenta and electric purple mixed
together, flowing in and out of each other.

Ashes

Empty me.
You empty me with every word you say.
I'm slowly falling apart
Locked within myself.
I'm slowly failing.

Twisting and turning
I'm sinking down
Your words tear me to pieces.
But I love you
You know that, right?
I love you to pieces.
I love you right down to the ash.

You turn me to ashes
With a look.

Empty me.
I empty myself with every move.
I'm slowly turning away
Hiding behind every wall,
I'm slowly dying.

Dropping and drowning
I'm jumping down

My movements tear me to pieces.
But I love you
You know that, right?
I love you to pieces
Right down to the ash.

You turn me to ashes
With a smile.

Survival

Everything aches.
Stalemate.
I can't move.
My body writhes
With the pain
Of past actions.
I'll never get rid of these scars.

I need so much
Just to survive.

Cut me with a rusty knife.
You see me as you see yourself:
A waste, pathetic and utterly complacent.

Cut me with a rusty knife,
Slit me open and watch me fall
Tear me down and look at my soul.

Empty me of pain.

I’m a fucking Princess too

How many girls will you ruin today?
How many will wish to look your way?
You’re the image showing starvation is right,
You’re the voice they all dream of at night.
You make little girls hate themselves.

You’re the pretty princess
Every girl wants to touch.
You’re unreachable,
But they want it so much.
All we feel for ourselves
Is guilt, shame and hate,
But you’re still in the castle
And I wish I hadn’t just ate.

Pretty pretty princess
Lined up in a row
Shoot them all down
And watch the lies flow

Mirror, mirror
On the wall
Who’s the fairest of them all?
It’s not you.
It’s not you.

Ballistic

They tell me I'm crazy,
That my mind is wrong.
I don't mean to be lazy,
I just don't belong.
Sharp, quick slashes,
There's hardly any pain.
My mistake flashes
An explosion in my brain.

Fuck this
I hate it
I just want to scream.
Going ballistic,
Wish I missed it,
I'm heading down.

My mind freezes suddenly,
I can't move at all.
The past is ahead of me,
I'm watching as I fall

Breathless

I want to cut, burn, sear you
Into me.
I ache for you and a way
To mark myself as yours.
My wrists throb,
Reminding me of a job unfinished.
You leave me breathless,
Needing more.
I always need more.

I crave you.
I carve me.
I carry you always.

Parts

How can I miss something
I've never touched with such an ache?
Every sentence in my head
Has you in it.
You make up the parts of me.
Your touch is all through me,
Your marks on my skin.
We make our own game
And share the rules with no one.
We sing our own song
In a language we patterned
After our hearts.
We beat together,
Always.

This is for you, it's only for you,
Always for you.
I hear you constantly, feel you watching me
Dangerously close to rhyme.
You do this to me.
And I beg for it.

Drown Me

My scars hurt
You're in my head.
I shiver, shake, want.
I stare at your words
And answer with my own.
This mad girl's love song.
This mad girl's aching pleading.
Covered with desperation, sadness
A want too large to bear.

I want to fall into you
My edges fray,
I need your razor.
This mad girl's coming
Apart at the seams.
She needs your needle and thread,
Your blackest stitches.
Your steady hand and gentle touch.

My pen bleeds you.
I can't stop this blizzard of words for you.
You leak out
Through my cracks,
Drown me.
Drown me.

Lancing

My head
                Sounds like this
Clunking lines
                Other's words
And I can never get warm.

Does everyone have these urges?
That
Little
Voice
That whispers
Step out into traffic
Jump off the station
Let the blade slip.
Do they all just ignore it
While I ignite?
I will fall and burn.
I will weep and bleed
I will let me dreams
Seep out through the seams
Hot and jaded
Oozing and festering
I must
Lance myself.

You stay

I don't know how I survived this long,
How I still draw breath,
Still beat,
When all I keep coming back to
Is destruction.
All I know for sure,
At the bottom,
Is you.
You stay, stuck.
Some part of you stays, always.
I can't scrub you out
And would never want to.
But I want to scour these walls
And rid myself of these
Destructive wants,
That drip down,
Ooze out,
Slip through
Until I'm covered in this
Pathetic self hatred,
Broken.
I want to scratch this pain out.
I want to scratch until I can't feel anymore.

Soothe

You teach me with your fingers.
They tap dance on my back,
A rhythm only I can hear.
I want to grasp you too tight,
I can't seem to believe you'll stay.
I feel time
Slipping,
Can feel something coming
That will rip us apart again.
I can't live through the distance
I can't live without your fingers
And their mindless rhythm.

When you're not here
I surround myself in you
To remind me you're not gone.
I listen to your voice for hours,
Your words soothe and sting in
Equal parts.
So much time lost already
And now we're running out.
I'm scared I'll lose you
Because I want you too much.

Every sad song

I can't get the last 12, 13, 14 years off my mind.
All this time, all my choices,
My mistakes.
I guess it's the time for memories.
I torture myself
With his voice, your voice
His words, your words.
Every sad song
You couldn't listen to.
I'm grieving a relationship
That is reborn.
Wishing the years
Could be reborn.

I don't know why those years
Pain me in this new way.
Even though we touch (finally)
My thoughts turn to other girls.
And whether I'm retracing
Someone else's fingertips.
If I measure up to
Your muscle memory,
To the others,
To the years.
I fear I'm found wanting,

That I've come too late.

I find myself wishing
I tried harder,
Stayed longer,
Not given up on you.
I feel sick when I think
Of the damage I did.
And I'm scared I'll somehow
Do it again.
And you're worried too.
But my words come up short,
I don't know how
To comfort you.
I don't know how
To explain the way
I'm connected to you,
The threads I could never sever,
Even when I wanted to.
That things inside me
Seek you out
In everything I do.
It's involuntary
I don't try to find you
Because you're already there,
A heart lengths away.
Always.

Blueberry

I remember when you kicked lazy circles.
Ran around.
Scattering smiles and laughter
Wherever you went.
Now you're reserved,
Quiet and anxious.
I don't know
How to get that back
Or if it's right
To want that back.
You will grow.
You will learn.
And you will
Overcome
In time.

Trapped

Enclosed in the fingers
Of obsession and addiction,
You tell me stories
Of you pain and misfortune.
But I don't care.
And I can smell her
Sitting in this room
Singing all her perfect songs
Perfectly out of tune.
But I don't mind.

Enclosed in the embrace
Of hurt and darkness
You yell about how
They love you less.
But I don't listen.
I can feel her
Lying down here
Kissing me pillows
Taking away my fear.
But I don't see.

Enclosed in the fingers
Of her and her loneliness
I hope you're happy
In the arms of emptiness.

I couldn't help it

I'm imperfect,
Insane, undone.
You yell and I sit,
Curl you round my tongue
And rip you in two.
Lick your wounds clean.
Stick you back together
Then I'll do it again.
I'll do it again.

And I flew
Straight into you.
You tore my wings in two.
And I crashed
Down on you.
You held on for a minute or two.
Then you ran.
You ran so far away.

I bled cause I knew it was over.
I bled cause I knew it was wrong.
I bled cause I knew it was over
And I knew we wouldn't belong.

I drew your picture in my mind

Pretended I was in love with you.
Why can't I get you out of my head?
What you promised wasn't true.

It's Not The Truth

Time flies when you're falling down
I can keep going or I can forget.
Burn it and let it all fall down.
I can't decide.
Lost in my thoughts,
It all combines into a mess
Of colours and sounds.
Nothing stands out.
She's wrapped in rags
Inside my head.
And I'll embrace her
Sharp caress.

I sing my tune of sadness
For myself.
They won't listen.
They say it hurts their ears.
They stand watching me.
They get inside my head.
They ruin my mind.
The tears are sour.
Bloodied and rotting.

Connection

A look,
A touch,
A note in your voice.
Our red thread
Of connection
Always there.

You are next to me
Failure isn't an option anymore.
Burn your doubts
Scatter the ashes
And give them up.
You wrap me up,
Tightly like a present,
And tuck me in,
Say goodnight.

Anxiety

It scratches at me,
Picking at the seams
Until I start to
Unravel.
My breath gets short, sharp, shallow.
My thoughts twirling,
I'm burning on the inside.

There's a lump in my chest,
It's heavy and
Won't move.
I try to breathe into it,
To see if it shrinks
But it doesn't twitch.

Dissolved

I'm a dissolved girl.
Dissolving into something more.
How far will I fall
Before someone stops me?
No one will know
If I never tell.
And I'll never tell.
It'll be gone before they get there.
Used to need and feel
I used to bleed
Now I'm unreal.
Screaming words I know too well.
No one hears,
But I don't care
Because I'm used to it
Being this way.

Y

Writing in the book she gave me
All my memories of you
Fit in a tiny box.
Everything tangible is burnt,
Gone away.
We didn't sing for years
And now you'll never sing again.
I don't know how to explain
The lost feelings,
The rewriting of history
In my mind.
If things had been different…
Maybe I wouldn't be here either.
You're in the back of my mind
All the time now.
"You're so vain" on tv
Memories of Newtown, images of fame.
You'll always be Candy to me.
The next Courtney.
What happened to make you give up
To throw away your dreams?
All questions, never answered.
Now I carry the dream for both of us
Afraid to fail and let you down.
Everything's reminding me of you.

I would've bled myself dry for you.
After all these years,
All this pain,
Every horrible thing
I'm still the same.
Now I can't do anything anymore.
Too scared.
Too hurt.
Too much trouble.
The stars just burn away.
You're with them now.
Just a memory
Held by so many.
How could you let yourself
fade away?

Fear

She cast out her fear
And I caught it, like a life jacket
Thrown to a drowning child.
I used it to stay afloat
On her sea of deception.
The waves crash over me
But I feel nothing.
She tried to save me,
Calling.
And I hear nothing.
Finally she gives up
And I’m left in her salty remains.

www.ingramcontent.com/pod-product-compliance
Lightning Source LLC
Chambersburg PA
CBHW051718130826
49812CB00034B/1245
* 9 7 8 9 3 5 7 2 1 1 8 5 7 *